Songs of the Viking Life

Reflections of a Frequent Flyer

Songs of the Viking Life

Reflections of a Frequent Flyer

by

James Taylor Pearson

First Edition: October 2015
Printed in the United States of America
ISBN: 978-1-682-73039-3

Dedicated to my Children

Taylor and Kathryn

Who sailed the skies with me always

And to my wonderful wife Laurie

Who made a new life possible

Front cover photo by Kathryn F. Pearson 2015 – Santorini, Greece

Back cover photos by Kathryn F. Pearson and James T. Pearson, 2015 – Bangalore, India; Dalian, China; Santorini, Greece

For information, email jim@tertiusvicus.com or visit TertiusVicus.com

Table of Contents

James Taylor Pearson

Preface

Get on the road. Make something great happen. Get paid. Repeat.

The Viking Life. In the last millennium it involved warfare and a great taking. Months away from home followed by a long winter of celebration. Now it is a weekly grind for millions of us – executives, salespersons, experts from all disciplines - just about anyone who must work far from home.

These songs and poems are the product of long hours in hotel rooms, airports, and conference rooms the world over. I hope you enjoy them.

Jim Pearson, Arlington

James Taylor Pearson

Chapter 1

Work

Clients Rule

On the beach
Beyond reach
        Of cellphones and loud shouts
But my boss
To my loss
        Has found my whereabouts

I'm running home
On the phone
        She explains her needs
The sand calls
My life stalls
        Children's time recedes

The Life that I Choose

To be read to the tune of "Sweet Baby James" by James Taylor

There is a consultant, who lives on a 'plane.
His phone and computer are his only companions.
He lives for the madness of client reactions,
Waiting for bonuses he'll never spend.

And as his phone rings he accesses his e-mail,
Thinkin' about spreadsheets (and glasses of beer).
Accepting commitments to do more BD work,
He thinks of friends who are no longer near,
And wonders if they'd like to hear:

"Hello, you Dot.Com Thousand-Aires, my colleagues whose net dreams went wrong;
Road warrior blues is the life that I choose,
So call on me when you need a friend,
And the new dreams we plan will be grand."

'Twas a Tuesday team dinner, in a Missouri
Mall,
He enters with colleagues and orders a beer.
He sits with the clients, and nods in agreement,
Knowing it's their own words that they like to
hear.

And as the talk wanders from projects to
pilsners
He thinks of his children and love left behind.
Pulling his mobile, he calls from the restaurant
And through the static they hear:

"Goodnight my rascally children,
Rockabye sweet Laurie Ann.
Road Warrior Blues is the life that I choose
I'll be home for you soon as I can.
And my love for you will never end."

Heathrow Transit

Inspired by Bobby Ferrin and our Friends at Heathrow

Your whole day in line was spent
And nothing good became of it
Don't worry
Be happy

Fourteen times your bag was checked
And now you can't lay hands on it
Don't worry
Be happy

You've learned smells you've never known
Most of them are your own
Don't worry
Be happy

Now you’re clear to fly away
But your flight left yesterday
Don't worry
Be happy

Monday

Monday
She comes in leaden boots
To set your alarm
Begging for attention
Demanding youth
No longer yours
To give

Office Politics

"Ich glaube das ein pherd mich tritt*"
Or perhaps I have just stepped in shit
My eyes not seeing an obvious hole
Or the actions of a corporate mole

** German colloquial for "I think a horse just kicked me". Loosely translates as "someone tricked me" or "you are pulling my leg".*

Detroit, MI
A Recession Casualty

Dead tooth.
Night grinding, pounding brings
Infection
Antibiotics
Dentist on the Road suggests
Root canals and crowns.

Banks fall, factories close, lawyers lay blame.
Teeth are ground out.

Not a great way to advance into the last years of
personal productivity
But to be expected in this town of hard drivers
When the stress gets political.

Reggae Woman

On Becoming a Regular in Strange City

Reggae woman
With golden 'dreds
Brings to me
My daily bread

In her eyes
A sea-blue smile
Upon her lips
A "Stay for a while"

The coffee pours
The words they flow
All too soon
I have to go

Reggae woman
With golden rings
Because of you
The city sings

Top 10 Signs You *Are* a Consultant

10.0 You lecture the neighborhood kids selling lemonade on ways to improve their processes.

9.0 You know the people at the airport airline club better than your last significant other.

8.0 You refer to the tomatoes grown in the community garden as deliverables.

7.0 You really do need a white board to explain yourself.

6.0 You eat dinner out of vending machines and at the most expensive restaurant in town within the same week.

5.0 You think Mother Theresa would have been more effective had she put her ideas into PowerPoint.

4.0 You get all excited when it is Sunday so you can wear sweats to work.

3.0 Your valet, limo service, and luggage repair-person are the first three auto-dial numbers on all four of your smartphones.

2.0 You are now learning the irregular verbs in her/his native language from the night janitor at the client's office.

1.0 You have outsourced our social planning to your friends. And they bill you.

0.5 You really wanted there to be a 0.5

Tears of Calgary: A Good Team

It does not rain in Calgary
Say the natives.
But it rained this week, all week
Steady, sniffling, heartbreaking, gray.
Tears of Calgary for those leaving
The team.

Robert, Deano, Andrea,
Long time pillars of our work.
Stephens Street will miss you.
Goodbye to Mango Shiva,
So long to Saltlik and Sukiyaki.
Like the ice and snow melt of April, the
Red wine no longer flows
For you.

All will be missed
At Jugo Juice, at Starbucks,
At the Executive Lounges.
The drums of the Zoo are silent.
The video conference rooms on the 17th floor
Will echo with empty sighs
As the Tears of Calgary bid you
Good bye.

April 15th with the Tax Accountant

May the long hours and revenues they drive
Bring summer vacation bliss
For certainly this Springtime pain
Pleads "Please, pay well for this"

Nightmares of an IT Purchaser

(Hum it to the tune of Tiny Bubbles)

Tiny Vendors
In a Garage
Promise anything
Including a Massage

Tiny Vendors
Give my hives all over
With the feelin' that they're gonna leave us
With a pile of Garbahge.

Washington D.C.
At the Old Ebbitt Grill

The anxious young men of Washington
Eyeing each other in the bar's soft green light.
Shall I swing left?
Shall I swing right?
In whose parlor shall I be listening tonight?

The anxious young men of Washington
Come into town with dreams burning bright
To serve morals that
Will not last the night
For it's power they seek in the bar's soft green light.

Vampire Economics

Companies bought with equities
Buried in debt, brought to their knees.
The Partner screams for added fees
Ladling on teams "with expertise".

Management, in their bids bested
Are replaced by the untested.
Irate investors clamor "More!"
Or this next batch is shown the door.

The goal is to bleed, not to build,
When it is done, all dreams are killed.
The Partners smile, add up their score,
While we weep for the newly poor.

The Coughs of Ishikawa-san

A very good client, a very good man

The coughs of Ishikawa-san
Launch tobacco's scent
Over my questioning face.

A long list of whys blow by
Why this smart man, why in this clean
city, why in this meeting?

Why do we allow the business of adding
chemicals
To nature's brown leaf?
Are politicians still bought that cheaply?
I don't see them smoking.

I like Ishikawa-san.
I am saddened today.

February Workin' Blues

My valentine candy's stolen
My kid's hamster she done died
Vet gave me stuff to keep her alive
And my how we tried and tried

I got them wintertime blues, MaMa
Rockin' my life away
Don't know if I'll get outta of bed
These blues they just gonna stay

The snow is black in Peoria
It's reached a hundred year height
Now it looks like I gotta drive
To Chicago to get to a flight

I got them Wintertime Blues, MaMa
Dragging me through the cold
Gotta get out to the heat and the sun
I'm just getting' too gray and old

Aphorisms from the Office

On Being (in the Workplace)

We always are what we always are.
Perhaps we just shouldn't push it
(Too often)
Too far.

Picking a Leader

Great people make the world.
Good people make it better.

Other People's Water

Water that flows from another's back
Should not dampen your spirits.

Nothing Beats an Educated Warrior

Nothing.

Haiku for the Road

Public and Private Worlds

Nightfall in Tokyo
Neon sewn Roppongi screams
Diet House whispers

Osaka City at 5am

Velvety black sky
Fireflies of light emerge
From sleepless windows

Stepping from the Bullet Train

Osaka morning
Angry buzz of black'n'white
Sal'ryman parade

Hanging in New York

New York lights glitter
Artful youth serves tradition
Don't dream it, be it

San Francisco Morning

Grey fogcats creeping
Curl around Coit, Candlestick,
Softly brush the dawn

Chapter 2

Life

No Whining

I want to say a muddle,
But truly I just dawdle,
Standing in a puddle
Leaking through my swaddle

But while not all is good
Nothing's too bad
And all that is wrong
Is 'cuz I'm a cad

So smile I do from time to time
And today I smile too
For all my cares turn 'round about
When I hear from you.

An Evening with Werner Herzog at the Kennedy Center

Werner showed wild in the rarified Center,
    Vines almost visible, growing to engulf us
    as he spoke his vision.

Where in Europe did he find his fascination with Amazonian spirits?
    The Old World likes to break a thing,
    whether nature or man. In him, Nature
    strikes back.

Werner will not sing for any man. Do not even ask.
    We hack at his jungle and cajole, watch and
    try to prize out meaning.

His jungle will not retreat.

In Praise of Bruce Springsteen

Inspired by 'Blinded by the Light'

a jack kerouac attack on a beach sunny sandy it should be fun but it is too much don't look behind-the-cabana 'cuz the clowns are real and their lives are very, very sad.   like these sometime nights.

all of us in suchahurry to crawl back from the office into the light of fun run, ride, hide, try to blend back into the cottoncandy crowd that does not see the adultonset trainwreck try to stay in neverland to believe all is great and grand no mentors-monsters slither under the boardwalk can we be just like a child wandersaunter too happy and unknowing and trying so veryvery hard to ignore not to see feel the pull of that beautyqueen to you or your emerging strongjawline to her.   but you can't.

suit up buck up get on another plane it won't kill you feeds the needs and keeps the kids on the beach – just out of reach.

Just get home before the clowns come out.

The Birthday Poem

Just what you want
A Birthday reminder.
I find forgetting
Infinitely kinder.

For Kids grow older
And we do not
Only smarter and faster,
If a bit shot.

Enjoy your day
And your family too
And as always in April
Happy Birthday to You.

Charlottesville, VA   Freshman Fall

Son turns to enter
His dorm, his new life.
Long hugs over
Feeling the Matrix
Unplug.

When We Dance

Bacchanals are for the young
For they have time to make good
The damage done

Inauguration 2005

The drums roll
The champagne flows
All hail the Might
Of the Right

The President speaks
The world awaits
All see the Might
Of the Right

Many poor joined the rich
        To make this choice
With their own hands
        Muzzled their voice
It is their Might
That lifts the Right

Tango de los Muertos Alemania

(Arguably to the Tune of "Don't Cry for Me, Argentina" from EVITA, by Lord Andrew Lloyd Webber. For my Argentinian friends on the eve of the 2014 World Cup Final)

It won't be easy, you'll think it strange,
When the Argentines destroy Germany,
While the Brazilian fans
    Yell down very harsh things

You won't believe it.
All you will see is the team you once thought
Was an invincible machine
Tango'd up on itself
    As the Bolas strike home.

Don't let me down Argentina!
Put sand in the Mannshaft of Deutchland!
Be wild and stealthy,
Streak to the goal line,
And show the Germans
    'Tango de los Muertos'!

Germany won the match, 1-0.

To My Love in the Season of Slanting Sunlight

To kiss your hand, my lips
Lovingly at ev'nings close
Wait, as passion grows

To kiss your cheek, my lips
Strengthening like archers' bows
Wait, as passion grows

To kiss your chin, my lips
Violently seeking the rose
Wait, as passion grows

To kiss your soul, my lips
Lost in effervescent throes
Wait, as passion grows.

Take Me Down

Drinkin' my coffee
Thinkin' hard about you
Things are heating up
Whatever shall I do?

Take me down,
Take me down to your river,
Cool me off,
Cool me in your water.

Razzin' in the sky,
Actress jawin' on the phone,
Hard to sleep while flying,
Never get back prone.

Day near gone, hotel room bare
I'm here thinkin', writin'
About a place with you, not here
Where my life is real, excitin'

Take me down,
Take me down to your river,
Cool me off,
Cool me in your water

Virginia Summer Golf

The rolling greens
The humid grass
The miss-hit drives
The goose's ass

Here again I come to play
Here again I come to pray

“May the ball fly
Straight and fine
May this putt
Find perfect line”

Not for me a perfect day
Come back again - again to pray

Report from the Starter's Shack
Late Fall, Greendale Golf Course

I hear the grasses sleeping.

Gentle rustling snores under a blanket of
browning leaves.
Dreams of summer sunrises, warming rains,
ambling players
Perplexed as the longer blades playfully hide
their soaring, slicing drives.

The grasses groan and shudder as they dream
Of the painful pinch when they are a part of a
perfect divot,
Followed by a contented sigh as they imagine
flight, freedom,
And landing to re-sod amidst a patch of new
friends.

Happy New Year!

So, in truth my brother,
I thought last year would be my nadir
but I have found that fates conspire
to rid me of illusion
and leave me flayed as this sad Winter
roars into March Madness.

I struggle daily, and only the promise
of release from this ruptured economy
gives my mind some peace.
Novels, movies, alcohol - too much of each and
all. I shall not mad behave nor go away
as too competitive I am.

But I weep. I weep hard for lost
futures. Poor decisions? I know not but that
I taste them, know them. They are mine.

I hope all is happy with you and yours
and work and future too.

To be at this place
At this time in life.
I should have it well built
and not be building still.

So pass the hoe and ale,
for in the fields I still must toil
as in my heart
my lost loves boil.
Is it always thus with youthful dreams?

Somewhere in Kansas
a girl looks at her ruby shoes
and has second thoughts.

DC Cherry Trees Bloom Late in 2013 due to Cold Spring

I think the blooms still are tryin'
To find their inner YoJah
So when they bloom all beautiful
They can say "I Told Yah"

Here in DC our trees don't speak
All subtle, smiling quiet
And yet when all the blooms come out
They are a freakin' riot

PBS

Presumptuous Broadcasting Services selling
Pedestrian BBC Serials,
Pre-chewed Bland Sentiments,
Prurient Boyish Sophistry, and
Pre-Thatcherite Brooding Sleuths to
Pretentious Britophilic Sycophants

Graduation and Reunion

1977 – Dreams of Youth

Oh Dad, won't you buy me a BMW?
I'm heading to college, and sinkin' Frats too.
I'll wear me five collars, and docksiders blue.
Oh Dad, won't you buy me a BMW?

2011 – Peak Foliage

Concierge, won't you hire me a stretch limousine?
I'm going to reunion, to see and be seen.
(Or perhaps a motor cycle, just like Steve McQueen)?
Concierge, won't you hire me a stretch limousine?

2041 – Karma

Oh Kids, won't you lend us your Mercedes Benz?
We're headin' to college with all our dear friends.
We'll drink lots of beer there, and wear our Depends.
Oh Kids, won't you lend us your Mercedes Benz?

My Daughter's First Day

She got out of the car and walked to the subway entrance.

She did not look back.

She had a lunch she had packed – herself.

A carryall bag she had filled – herself.

Going to a job, her first in the City, that she had found and landed

Herself.

I am in awe. I am in tears. I am very, very proud.

Experiencing through Haiku

The Great Why

Eve look'd on Adam
We their children, wiser now,
Question her judgment

Envy

Little Mini Coop
Dreams of being Mercedes
The Kia blushes

The Turning of the S^UV^crew

Gliding to office
Toyotas smile, free ranging,
Hunting Escalades

Unfair World

Swan, angelic, smiles
Spring's new eyes seek her glory
Molting ducks cry foul

Egypt

Naguib Mahfouz shouts
Sons and daughters of Pharaoh
Deserve their freedom

Ambition

Somewhere at Yale lay
Pictures of Bill, Hill, and W.
Naked, and wanting.

According to news accounts: Students entering Yale from the 1940's to the 1960's were required to be photographed naked for a study of posture and personality.

Brief Thoughts on Searing Pain
September 11, 2001

Great Nation awaking
Notorious winds from far
Our people aflame

Four times, four death ships
With innocent lives they kill
Thousands of dreams lost

Fall spirit challenged
Flames scorch, leave ashes and scars
The phoenix will rise

Many differences
All arrogance swept aside
One spirit remains

A flag once forgot
In the fall of cynicism
Proudly flying now

September 11, 2001

In the Season of Clouded Sun

Splendid Sequoia
Strong with life, fall together.
All the world hears

In the Season of Violent Winds

Fifty nations lose
Their friends, their souls, tragedy.
Falwell blames the free

In the Season of Uniting Spirits

Pentagon, mighty
Nation's home base, heroes of
Fall rebuild, prepare

Reflections on 9/11/2001

Now leaves tumble by
Will the harsh sting of autumn
Bring barren winter?

Authored by my Father, Melvin E. Pearson, the first Operations Officer of the first US Navy SEAL Team

Chapter 3

Balance

A Very Good Month

October 2014

I have enjoyed the fullness of this October
Every day I did a little something
I really wanted to do.

It was an inestimable pleasure.

A Good Book

A leisurely search
A cover seen, checked out
A weekend's joy
The soul revives

The best stories
Act like a healer's poultice
To draw out sorrow
And replace it with wonder

Now We Are 50
(With apologies to A.A. Milne)

Now We Are 50
Our dreams to winds blown
The seeds that we planted
Have died or have grown.

The children, the lovers,
The street passers-by
Have thanked us, hugged us,
And said their goodbyes.

Time to lie down
Our work here is through;
Time to wake up
And shake off youth's dew.

Been there? Done that?
Want to again?
Crawl out to re-find
Our dearest old friends.

Pull out shared memories
Torn from times gone;
Re-open our hearts
And sing forth a new dawn.

Letting Go

When our years are passed well over
And our hairs sprout up all grey
It's time to tell the pretty young ones
To simply go away.

No matter how they chase us
All the live long day
We must simply let them know
That it's time to go away.

Go chat up their Mommas
And listen when they say:
"Just let the little darlings
Know it's time to go away.

"Tell them you've lived with stress and worry -
Youthful games bring hell to pay -
Tell them what you must!
Then tell them 'Go Away'".

No matter how they argue
No matter how they pray
Sincerely thank them gently,
Then simply walk away.

Reflections at a Fishing Village
Santorini, Greece

Climbing the Caldera or awash in the salty clear
Aegean,
The Goddess Abundance lifts civilization from
the plow, the net, and the line
The Gods of War, Tempest, and Harvest, who
rely on our fear,
Are tempered with Wisdom, Poetry, Song (and
Wine).
Theaters are built, lives devoted to thought and
provocation.
Ancient drains in the seats of the Nobility allow
for long festivals where they watch
themselves set alight.
Plays, poems, and music challenge thought as
well as entertain, bring down empires and
Gods alike,
Leaving us to discover ourselves in their
shadow and in their light.

Abundance inspires Theater
Theater inspires Wisdom
Wisdom inspires Humanity.

Rounding the Turn

Golfing after the Rain

Rainbows dance on the greens as the
Sun comes up and strikes the dew.
Small balls bounce leaving little rips
And pockmarks as they head towards home.

Wet shoes kick droplets that sparkle as they
Land on the fairway - or in the rough.
Smiles alight upon the faces of everyone
Blessed to be here on an October morning.

Balancing

Yin Seeking

Falling waters filled
With freckled sun, enticing
Yang spirit onward

View from the Library Window

Riding the Spring Wind
Cherry petals, a blizzard
of kisses, bring smiles

Summer in Chicago

Bold sun commands wind
Bent trees worship her and make
Cool Exhalations

New England Autumn

Fall spills in slowly
Indian summer stores heat
For our Winter hearts

Mid-Atlantic Autumn

Ivy leaves float lonely
Down, beautiful agony
of Fall, joy to life

Pacific Northwest Autumn

Late berries push forth
Sweetening the coming Fall
With scented breezes

Autumn On the 18th Tee

Mist on the tee box
In the haze deer graze, leaves blaze
A wolf comes stalking

Chapter 4

In Memoriam

For Kyle and Eric

Brothers in my life
Brothers to me
Designed for a different destiny

Whole worlds you made
Whole worlds your own
Into them you now have gone

These worlds created
These worlds we shared
What shall now we do

Knowing you are not there

Voices

I hear voices
In the droplets
At the memorial fountain of the Center for
Hope.

'Happy Birthday', 'I Love You',
Shouting about the unpaid bills.
The names on the benches
Speak to the names on the bricks.

"What did the Doctor say?"
"Should we tell him?"
Whispers in the hallways,
Smiles in the patient suite,
Tears in the parking lot.

I love you.
I care for you.
We will always, always
Remember you.

Remembering a Leader

Blazer hanging familiar in the sun,
White hair shading reading eyes.
Volvo parked casually in the entry
It's selection today giving away something: a new client,
Or the only car company you have not yet served?

Looking cowboy-eyed into the sky,
Smoke escapes while the magazine hand dips slowly.
Eyes back to reading, thoughts to building
The insights that shape the world.
An intellectual in a dirty fingernail firm;
The last person to make smoking look good.

For Allen

Friends hold hands, crying
Your pain too much, you deserve
Incandescent joy

For Robin Williams

Life without Robin
    will be a darker place.
No more peekaboo with 15 of your best friends
    and 101 new ones you are excited to meet.
No more thoughtful looks that break into a smile
    itself undecided on breaking.

No more sense that there is someone who has
    eaten the world
And from whom shines the light of every
    person, every culture, every practice
Accepted, acknowledged, with laughter bringing
    us all to a place of peace

And forgiveness.

Thank you

A New Year's Wish

When mud arose to see skies blue
It offered up a big "Thank You"

We thank you for our daily bread,
We thank you for the tears we've shed
We thank you for our coats and shoes
We thank you for our joys and blues.

For life together, so sweet and true,
And for the years to come, we say

Thank you

For more information, please visit
TertiusVicus.com or email
jim@tertiusvicus.com.